3/05

# Presidents

Written by Chris Oxlade
Illustrated by Mike White

p

This is a Parragon Publishing Book
First published in 2000

Parragon Publishing
Queen Street House
4 Queen Street
Bath BA1 1HE, UK

ISBN 0-75254-643-0

Printed in Singapore

Produced by
Monkey Puzzle Media Ltd
Gissing's Farm
Fressingfield
Suffolk IP21 5SH
UK

Designer: Sarah Crouch
Cover design: Victoria Webb
Editor: Linda Sonntag
Editorial assistance: Lynda Lines
and Eileen Ramchandran
Indexer: Caroline Hamilton
Artwork commissioning:
Roger Goddard-Coote
Project manager: Alex Edmonds

# Contents

### What is the president's job?

The president is in charge of the United States of America. His list of jobs includes being head of the government administration and foreign policy. He chooses people to head government departments (the Secretaries of State, the Treasury, Defense, and so on), and he is Commander-in-Chief of the U.S. Army and U.S. Navy.

### What is the Oval Office?

The Oval Office is the President's private office in the West Wing of the White House. It was added to the White House in 1909.

### Who can be president?

You have to be at least 35 years old, a natural citizen of the U.S., and you must have lived in the U.S. for at least 14 years. Of course, you have to be elected too!

# Where does the president live?

THE PRESIDENT'S OFFICIAL HOME ADDRESS IS 1600 PENNSYLVANIA AVENUE, Washington, D.C., commonly known as the White House. As well as private rooms for the president and his family, the White House also has dozens of public function rooms and government offices. All of the presidents have lived at the White House, since 1800 when the second president, John Adams, and his wife Abigail, moved in.

### What is a presidential term?

The time that a president stays in office. A term always begins at noon on January 20, when one president steps down and the new president is inaugurated. The term ends exactly four years later.

The White House was burnt down during the British invasion in 1814 but rebuilt in the 1820s.

### Who chooses the president?

The people of the U.S.! In the November of the year before a presidential term ends, the people in each state vote for people called electors. The electors then vote for the presidential candidates from each political party. The candidate who gains the majority of votes wins.

### How long can a person be president?

The maximum time that a president can serve for is two complete terms, or eight years. Then he must step down. The rule was introduced in 1951.

### What does the vice-president do?

The vice-president is elected along with the president as his "running mate"—a sort of second-in-command. The vice-president acts as president of the Senate, and takes over as president for the rest of the term if the president dies.

The president's airplane has to be very secure as well as having the latest technology to keep the president in touch with his staff.

### Who is the first lady?

The first lady is the president's wife. Traditionally, she organizes functions and acts as hostess at the White House. She also becomes involved in social issues and charities.

### Will there ever be a first man?

There's no reason why not, since there's nothing to prevent a woman from becoming president.

# What is Air Force One?

THE AIRPLANE THAT THE PRESIDENT AND THE WHITE HOUSE STAFF USE WHEN THEY travel on official business. Air Force One is operated by the U.S. Air Force, and is currently a Boeing 747.

# Who was the first president?

GEORGE WASHINGTON WAS ELECTED FIRST PRESIDENT IN 1789. WASHINGTON led the Continental army against the British during the American Revolution, after which the United States was formed and became an independent country. Washington was president for two terms in office. He died in 1799.

Washington declined a third term as president.

### Which presidents were also vice-presidents?
Adams, Jefferson, Van Buren, Nixon, Ford, and Bush, who were later elected president, and Tyler, Fillmore, Andrew Johnson, Arthur, Theodore Roosevelt, Coolidge, Truman, and Lyndon Johnson, who took over on the death of the president.

### Which president was never elected?
Gerald Ford. He became vice-president in 1973 when Vice-president Agnew resigned. He became President Ford in 1974 when President Nixon himself resigned.

### Which president lost but won?
In the 1888 election, only 48% of the people voted for Benjamin Harrison versus 49% for his opponent Grover Cleveland. But more electors voted for Harrison, and he won by 233 to 168.

### How many presidents have there been?

Up to and including Bill Clinton, there have been 42 presidents of the U.S. They are ...

| | | |
|---|---|---|
| 1 | 1789 | George Washington (1732—1799) |
| 2 | 1797 | John Adams (1735—1826) |
| 3 | 1801 | Thomas Jefferson (1743—1826) |
| 4 | 1809 | James Madison (1751—1836) |
| 5 | 1817 | James Monroe (1758—1831) |
| 6 | 1825 | John Quincy Adams (1767—1848) |
| 7 | 1829 | Andrew Jackson (1767—1845) |
| 8 | 1837 | Martin Van Buren (1782—1862) |
| 9 | 1841 | William Henry Harrison (1773—1841) |
| 10 | 1841 | John Tyler (1790—1841) |
| 11 | 1845 | James Knox Polk (1795—1849) |
| 12 | 1849 | Zachary Taylor (1784—1849) |
| 13 | 1850 | Millard Fillmore (1800—1874) |
| 14 | 1853 | Franklin Pierce (1804—1869) |
| 15 | 1857 | James Buchanan (1791—1868) |
| 16 | 1861 | Abraham Lincoln (1809—1865) |
| 17 | 1865 | Andrew Johnson (1808—1875) |
| 18 | 1869 | Ulysses Simpson Grant (1822—1885) |
| 19 | 1877 | Rutherford Birchard Hayes (1822—1893) |
| 20 | 1881 | James Abram Garfield (1831—1881) |
| 21 | 1881 | Chester Alan Arthur (1830—1886) |
| 22 | 1885 | Grover Cleveland (1837—1908) |
| 23 | 1889 | Benjamin Harrison (1833—1901) |
| 24 | 1893 | Grover Cleveland (1837—1908) |
| 25 | 1897 | William McKinley (1843—1901) |
| 26 | 1901 | Theodore Roosevelt (1858—1919) |
| 27 | 1909 | William Howard Taft (1857—1930) |
| 28 | 1913 | Woodrow Wilson (1856—1924) |
| 29 | 1921 | Warren Gamaliel Harding (1865—1923) |
| 30 | 1923 | Calvin Coolidge (1872—1933) |
| 31 | 1929 | Herbert Clark Hoover (1874—1964) |
| 32 | 1933 | Franklin Delano Roosevelt (1882—1945) |
| 33 | 1945 | Harry S Truman (1884—1972) |
| 34 | 1953 | Dwight David Eisenhower (1890—1969) |
| 35 | 1961 | John Fitzgerald Kennedy (1917—1963) |
| 36 | 1963 | Lyndon Baines Johnson (1908—1973) |
| 37 | 1969 | Richard Milhous Nixon (1913—1994) |
| 38 | 1974 | Gerald Rudolph Ford (1913—) |
| 39 | 1977 | James Earl Carter (1924—) |
| 40 | 1981 | Ronald Wilson Reagan (1911—) |
| 41 | 1989 | George Herbert Walker Bush (1924—) |
| 42 | 1993 | William Jefferson Clinton (1946—) |

Under Van Buren, the U.S. went to war with the Seminole Indians.

# Who was the first all-American president?

MARTIN VAN BUREN WAS THE FIRST PRESIDENT born as an American citizen. The presidents before him were born before the Declaration of Independence in 1776, and so were officially British citizens.

Theodore Roosevelt won the Nobel Peace Prize in 1905 for trying to help resolve the Russo-Japanese war.

# Who was the youngest president?

## THEODORE ROOSEVELT, THE 26TH PRESIDENT. HE WAS ELECTED

vice-president in the 1900 elections and became president in September 1901 after the assassination of President McKinley. He was just 42 years old at the time. He was easily reelected for a second term in 1904.

### Who was the oldest president?

Ronald Reagan, who was 69 years old when he was inaugurated in January 1981. Reagan was reelected in 1984, and was 77 when he left office in 1989.

### Who was president most briefly?

The 9th president, William Henry Harrison. He was in office from March 4 to April 4, 1841. Harrison was 68 years old when he was inaugurated, and died from pneumonia exactly one month later.

### Who was reelected the most times?

Franklin Delano Roosevelt was the only president to be elected three times (1932, 1936, and 1940), and he was elected again (1944) to make a record four times.

### Who was elected again after defeat?
President Grover Cleveland is the only president to have served two terms separated by another presidency (that of Benjamin Harrison).

### Who was the youngest elected president?
John F. Kennedy was elected as president in 1961 at the age of 44. He narrowly defeated Richard Nixon in the election.

### Which presidents resigned?
Only President Richard Nixon, on August 9, 1974, halfway through his second term. He resigned because of the Watergate affair.

### Which state have most presidents come from?
Virginia, where eight presidents have been born, including four of the first five. Next comes Ohio, with seven. President Clinton was the first president from Arkansas.

Franklin D. Roosevelt lost the use of his legs as a result of the illness, polio, in 1921.

# Who was president longest?

FRANKLIN DELANO ROOSEVELT, WHO HELD OFFICE FOR MORE than 12 years. He was elected in 1932 and again in 1936. In 1940 he became the first and only president to be elected for a third term. In 1944 he was elected again, but died suddenly in office in 1945. This was before the presidency was restricted to two terms.

The CIA was linked with the Watergate scandal and was criticized by many people.

# Who started the CIA?

THE CIA (CENTRAL INTELLIGENCE AGENCY) WAS FORMED DURING THE administration of President Harry S. Truman in 1947. Its job is to collect and interpret information about other countries. In the past it has been accused of interfering in the internal affairs of countries, including the U.S..

**Who signed salt for peace?**
SALT is short for Strategic Arms Limitation Talks. These were negotiations between the United States and the former Soviet Union to stop production of nuclear missiles. SALT I (1972) was signed by President Nixon and Soviet leader Leonid Brezhnev. SALT II (1979) was signed by Leonid Brezhnev and President Carter.

# Who made the U.S. twice as big?

In 1803, President Jefferson agreed to buy an area of land known as the Louisiana Territory from France. It stretched from the Mississippi River to the Rocky Mountains, and cost just $15 million.

### Which president helped abolish slavery?

Abraham Lincoln. Slavery was the main reason for the Civil War (1861—1865), between the northern states (the Unionists), which wanted slavery abolished, and the southern states (the Confederates), which wanted to keep it. Lincoln was president of the victorious Union during the war.

### Who invented the cabinet?

The cabinet is a committee made up of the heads of the government departments. It was George Washington's idea. Originally it had just four members—the secretaries of State, the Treasury, War, and the Attorney General.

### Who was the Great Conservationist?

Theodore Roosevelt, the 26th president. He warned people about the dangers of using up the world's natural resources, and established the first wildlife refuge at Pelican Island, Florida.

### Who had a hotline to Russia?

In the early 1960s, President Kennedy called for an end to the Cold War between the West, led by the United States, and the East, led by the former Soviet Union (often called Russia). A special telephone line was connected between the White House and the Kremlin, the residence of the Soviet leader, so that the leaders could talk in times of crisis.

Jefferson was a very good scholar and was the main writer of the Declaration of Independence.

**Who lost the White House in 1812?**

The War of 1812 (which lasted from 1812 to 1815) was fought between the United States and Britain. In 1814, President James Madison fled from the White House before it was captured and burned out by the British.

**Who reinforced the East Coast?**

In 1823, President James Monroe announced that the United States would not put up with any more European interference in America. He supervised construction of a chain of defenses on the East Coast of the United States to resist invasions.

# Which president led a revolution?

## BEFORE BECOMING THE FIRST PRESIDENT OF THE UNITED STATES,

George Washington was an army officer. In the War of Independence against the British, General Washington led the Continental army, which he turned from a band of farmers into a fighting force. After five years of fighting, the turning point of the war came in 1781, when the main British force surrendered at Yorktown.

Washington was a distinguished soldier who co-ordinated his generals well against the British.

Andrew Jackson became a hero after defeating the British at New Orleans.

### Who won a war with Mexico?

James Knox Polk. He was president during the Mexican War (1846—1848), and fought over the position of the border between Mexico and the United States. The United States won half of Mexico.

### When were there two presidents?

During the Civil War (1861—1865), 11 states left the United States (the Union) to form the Union of Confederate States (the Confederacy). Abraham Lincoln was president of the Union, and Jefferson Davis was president of the Confederacy.

# Which hero was called hickory?

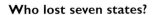

ANDREW "OLD HICKORY" JACKSON. AS MAJOR General Jackson, he led a force of volunteers to victory against the Creek Indians in 1814, and also defeated the British in the Battle of New Orleans in 1815.

### Who lost seven states?

James Buchanan, who was president before Abraham Lincoln. Near the end of his presidency, the states of Alabama, Florida, Georgia, Louisiana, Mississippi, South Carolina, and Texas left the Union before the start of the Civil War.

### ... and who got them back?

Abraham Lincoln, president of the victorious Union side during the Civil War (1861—1865). He was assassinated a few days after the war ended.

### Who declared war on Spain?

The 25th president, William McKinley. He declared war on Spain in 1898 because the Spanish would not leave Cuba. The United States won the war after defeating Spain in sea and land battles.

In the attack on Pearl Harbor, 2,400 people were killed, and 300 aircraft and 18 ships were destroyed.

### Who declared war in 1917?

President Woodrow Wilson ordered U.S. ships to be armed against attacks by German submarines in March 1917. War was declared the following month.

### Who dropped the nuclear bomb on Japan?

Harry S. Truman took over as president in 1945, when World War II was still being fought. Truman authorized two nuclear bombs to be dropped on Japanese cities to force the Japanese to surrender quickly.

# Who led the U.S. into World War II?

JAPAN ATTACKED THE U.S. NAVAL BASE AT PEARL HARBOR, HAWAII, IN 1941.

Franklin D. Roosevelt was president at the time. The United States immediately declared war. Roosevelt was president and Commander-in-Chief of the U.S. armed forces until he died shortly before the end of war.

### What was the Bay of Pigs?
In 1961, President Kennedy approved a plan for the CIA to help Cuban refugees invade Cuba and overthrow communist leader Fidel Castro. The invasion failed at the Bay of Pigs on Cuba's southern coast.

### Who ended the crisis in Cuba?
In 1963, there were rumors that the Soviet Union was putting nuclear missiles on Cuba. The Soviets withdrew when President Kennedy promised that the U.S. would not invade Cuba.

### Who stayed away from the Olympics?
After the Soviet Union invaded Afghanistan in 1979, President Carter protested by ordering a boycott of the 1980 Moscow Olympics. Sixty-three other nations joined the boycott and refused to attend.

### Who made war in the Gulf?
After Iraqi forces invaded Kuwait in 1990, President Bush announced operation Desert Shield to protect neighboring countries in the Persian Gulf. In 1991, U.S. troops led operation Desert Storm to recapture Kuwait.

# Who sent troops to Vietnam?

IN THE MID 1960S, PRESIDENT JOHNSON SENT NEARLY HALF A MILLION TROOPS TO South Vietnam to fight against communist attacks from North Vietnam. The troops were withdrawn by President Nixon in the early 1970s.

### Who shot down a U-2?
During the Cold War, a U-2 spy plane of the U.S. Air Force was shot down over the Soviet Union with its pilot Francis Gary Powers. President Eisenhower defended the flight, saying that it was necessary for national security.

### Who became president in a plane?
Lyndon B. Johnson took over as president when President Kennedy was assassinated in Dallas in 1963. Johnson took the oath of office on board Air Force One in Dallas before returning to Washington, D. C.

Images on television showed the people of the U.S. the true horror of what was happening in Vietnam, and the war became very unpopular.

Bill Clinton with his wife, Hillary, and their daughter, Chelsea.

# What was Whitewater?

IN 1993, PEOPLE SAID THAT MONEY HAD BEEN ILLEGALLY GIVEN TO THE Whitewater Land Development Corporation. President Bill Clinton and the first lady, Hillary Clinton, were part owners of the company at the time and were therefore involved in the case.

### Which president had too much of his own way?
Andrew Jackson. In 1834, he was told off by the Senate for "dictatorial and unconstitutional behavior" after he took government money from the Bank of America and put it in smaller state banks.

### What is impeachment?
Impeachment is the process of bringing legal charges against the president. The Senate acts as a court of law and tries the president.

### What was the Iran-Contra scandal?
When Ronald Reagan was president, it was discovered that government officials had secretly been selling weapons to Iran. They used the profits from the sales to help Contra rebels in Nicaragua, who were fighting against the Communist regime in the country.

# What was Watergate?

A POLITICAL SCANDAL THAT HAPPENED IN 1972, WHEN REPUBLICAN RICHARD Nixon was president. Five men were arrested after breaking into the rival Democratic party headquarters in the Watergate building in Washington, D.C., with electronic equipment for tapping telephones. It was found that staff from the White House had planned the break-in and organized a cover-up with Nixon's approval. Nixon resigned in August 1974 because of the scandal.

### Has a president ever been impeached?
Yes, but only one. He was 17th president, Andrew Johnson. He was impeached in 1868 for sacking his Secretary of War without the consent of the Senate. He was found not guilty by the Senate.

### Who has Congress tried to impeach?
Attempts have been made to impeach three presidents (in addition to Andrew Johnson). They are John Tyler, Richard Nixon, and Bill Clinton.

### Whose administration was corrupt?
Warren Harding's. He was president from 1921 to 1923. The worst money scandal during this time was the "Teapot Dome," in which Secretary of the Interior Albert Falls gave companies the right to drill for oil in return for money.

Nixon made his resignation speech on television. In 1974, he was pardoned for his part in the scandal by Gerald Ford.

# Who shot President Kennedy?

LEE HARVEY OSWALD ... PROBABLY. PRESIDENT KENNEDY WAS SHOT AND killed while driving in a motorcade through Dallas on November 22, 1963. Lee Harvey Oswald, a former marine and a communist, denied firing the gun, but was shot himself before he could be tried. Many people believe that Oswald was not the killer, or at least he did not act alone.

## Who shot Kennedy's killer?
Two days after President Kennedy was killed, Lee Harvey Oswald was shot at point-blank range by night-club owner Jack Ruby. Oswald was being moved to prison at the time.

## What happens if a president dies in office?
The vice-president is immediately sworn in as president. The new president then selects a new vice-president.

Nobody really knows who Jack Ruby was and why he killed Lee Harvey Oswald, but there are many theories.

## Is there a new election after a president's death?
No. The vice-president is elected in partnership with the president, and voters know that he could become president. He serves for the remainder of the presidential term.

## Were any other presidents assassinated?
James Garfield and William McKinley. Garfield was shot on July 2, 1881, at Baltimore and Potomac station in Washington, D.C. He died two months later from blood poisoning caused by operations to remove the bullet. McKinley was shot on September 6, 1901, and died eight days later from gangrene.

## Has a president been shot and survived?
Yes. Two in fact—Andrew Jackson and Ronald Reagan. In 1835, a man fired two guns at Jackson, but neither discharged. Jackson was lucky because both weapons were later found to be in working order. In 1981, John Hinckley shot Reagan in the chest. Reagan was lucky to survive.

Just five days after Lincoln's victory in the Civil War, he was murdered.

# Which president was shot in a theater?

ABRAHAM LINCOLN, THE 16TH PRESIDENT, ON APRIL 14, 1865, AT FORD'S Theater, Washington, D.C. He died the next day. Lincoln was shot from behind while watching the stage from his box. His assassin, John Wilkes Booth, leapt onto the stage, shouting "The South is avenged!" (He was referring to the Civil War, in which the South was defeated.) Booth was shot and killed resisting arrest two days later.

### Which president survived a duel?
Andrew Jackson. In a duel in 1806 with Charles Dickinson, a local lawyer, Jackson was shot in the chest. The bullet was never removed. Dickinson died in the duel.

### Which other presidents died in office?
Four presidents died of natural causes. They were William Henry Harrison, Zachary Taylor, Warren G. Harding, and Franklin D. Roosevelt.

# What was Ronald Reagan's first job?

FROM 1932, THE 40TH PRESIDENT WAS A BASEBALL AND FOOTBALL RADIO announcer. In 1937, he got an acting contract and by 1965 he had made more than 50 feature films.

Before he began his political career, Ronald Reagan was an actor. Here he is in 1951, posing with his co-star in the film *Bedtime for Bonzo*.

### Who could have been a pro football player?
George Bush. As a senior at the University of Michigan, he was named Most Valuable Player on the Michigan Wolverines football team. In 1935, he played for the College All-Stars team against the Chicago Bears. Soon afterward, both the Detroit Lions and Green Bay Packers offered him contracts.

### Who overcame a learning disability?
Woodrow Wilson, who at nine years old could still not read or do his arithmetic. He also had bad eyesight and poor health. But he was a great success at college.

Since he was defeated by Reagan in the 1980 election, Carter has been heavily involved in promoting human rights issues.

### Which president dressed to impress?

Martin Van Buren. He had a small, solid figure, a balding head with long white hair, and flowing sideburns. He was always perfectly dressed, and was once described as "exquisite in appearance." Van Buren was often criticized in the newspapers for being too interested in what he wore.

### Who refused to lie about a cherry tree?

George Washington—but the story is probably a myth. It was claimed that as a child Washington owned up to cutting down his father's cherry tree, saying that he could not tell a lie.

### Where did Theodore Roosevelt work for the police?

In New York City. From 1895 to 1897, Roosevelt served as president of the New York City Police Board. He rooted out corruption and enforced a ban on the sale of alcohol on Sundays.

### Who sent food to Belgium?

Herbert Hoover, who was head of the American Relief Committee and the Commission for the Relief of Belgium after World War I. He sent 34 million tons of food, clothes and supplies to the people of Europe.

### Who worked as a translator aged just 14?

John Quincy Adams, who was president from 1825—1829. He lived in Europe as a child and by the age of 14 he could speak fluent French. He was chosen as secretary to an American politician working in St. Petersburg, Russia.

# Which president grew peanuts?

JIMMY CARTER, WHOSE FAMILY RAN A PEANUT FARM IN GEORGIA. CARTER TOOK over the business after the death of his father in 1953. Before this, he was a submarine officer.

General Taylor had little formal education, but was a well-respected soldier. He was only in office for 16 months.

## Who made a lucky escape from the French?

During the French and Indian War (1753—1760), George Washington fought in the Virginia Militia. At Pittsburgh, four bullets went through his clothes and two horses were killed as he rode them.

## Who won the Battle of New Orleans?

Andrew Jackson. During the War of 1812 (1812—1815), Jackson's troops defended the city against highly-trained British troops. Two thousand British troops were killed or injured, compared to just 21 Americans.

## Who led the Union army in the Civil War?

Ulysses S. Grant. In 1862, he won the first major victory of the war against the Confederates, and was promoted to major general. After more victories he was made commander of all the Union armies in 1864.

## Who rode rough at Kettle Hill?

The Rough Riders was a cavalry regiment made up of volunteers. They were formed in 1898 to fight in the Spanish-American War. At Kettle Hill, Cuba, they made a brave charge, led by Colonel Theodore Roosevelt.

## Who was the youngest pilot in the navy?

In 1943, George Bush earned his wings to become the youngest pilot in the navy. He flew 58 sorties in torpedo bombers against Japanese ships in the Pacific. He was shot down twice at sea, and won the Distinguished Flying Cross.

# Who made his name fighting Mexicans?

ZACHARY TAYLOR, WHO FOUGHT IN THE MEXICAN WAR (1846—1848). IN 1847, at Buena Vista, General Taylor's men fought and beat a much larger force of Mexicans. During the battle, two bullets went through Taylor's clothing. Taylor became a hero when news of the victory reached Washington. He later became the 12th president.

# What did Eisenhower plan in Europe?

DWIGHT D. EISENHOWER JOINED THE ARMY DURING WORLD WAR I AND SERVED until 1948. In 1943, during World War II, he became a general and was given the title of Supreme Allied Commander. He was ordered to plan Operation Overlord, the Allied invasion of Europe, which began with the D-day landings in France on June 6, 1944.

### Why did Kennedy get a Purple Heart?

John F. Kennedy was commander of a patrol boat that was sliced in two by a Japanese destroyer in World War II. He swam to an island, towing an injured crewman with him. He was awarded a Purple Heart medal for bravery.

### Who beat the Shawnee Indians at Tippecanoe?

The Battle of Tippecanoe Creek took place in 1811. William Henry Harrison, then Governor of Indiana, with a force of army regulars and militiamen fought off a surprise attack by 700 Shawnees.

After military success in World War II, as president, Eisenhower used his skills to try to solve the Cold War situation.

# What did 70 million people watch?

THE FIRST TELEVISED ELECTION DEBATE BETWEEN JOHN F. KENNEDY AND RICHARD Nixon, who were opponents in the 1960 presidential election campaign. They appeared together on four live television debates. An incredible 70 million people watched the first debate.

### Who had a tough job in Great Britain?

John Adams was appointed ambassador to Britain in 1785, just two years after America's independence was recognized. It was a tough job because he was the first ambassador, and there were still bad feelings between the countries. Adams returned to the United States in 1788, soon to be elected vice-president.

James Polk may have been little known, but he was said to have brought about the Mexican War with his aggressive policies.

# Who asked, "Who is James Polk?"

WHEN THE DEMOCRATS TRIED TO CHOOSE THEIR MAN for the 1844 presidential election, they found it impossible to decide between the candidates. Then James K. Polk entered the race and won. He was so little known that during the elections, members of the Whig party made fun of him, asking, "Who is James Polk?"

The idea of two politicians debating on television caught the imagination of the U.S.

**When was the Republican Party founded?**
In 1854. Its first president was Abraham Lincoln. Between 1860 and 1928 all but two presidents were Republicans.

**Which rich man pretended to live in a log cabin?**
So that people would vote for him, William Henry Harrison's supporters portrayed him as a man of few means, who lived in a small log cabin and drank cheap cider. In fact, he lived in luxury in a 22-room manor house.

**... and the Democratic Party?**
The Democratic party was formed in the 1790s. Confusingly, its members called themselves Republicans at first.

**Who were the mugwumps?**
Mugwumps were Republicans who deserted their own candidate James Blaine to help the campaign of Democrat Grover Cleveland, who was elected president in 1884.

**Who was the brains behind the Brains Trust?**
The Brains Trust was a team of top advisors gathered together by Franklin D. Roosevelt. It helped him to win the 1932 election.

**Have all presidents been either Republicans or Democrats?**
No. The Federalist party was supported by the first two presidents, George Washington and John Adams. In the mid-1800s, the Whigs had four presidents—William Henry Harrison, John Tyler, Zachary Taylor, and Millard Fillmore.

# Which first lady is most famous?

Jackie Kennedy, later Onassis, was always in the media spotlight. She was a glamorous woman who was loved by the people of the U.S.

IT MUST BE JACQUELINE LEE BOUVIER (1929—1994), WHO BECAME MRS. KENNEDY. She met John F. Kennedy in 1951, and they were married in 1953. After her husband's assassination, she married Greek shipping tycoon Aristotle Onassis in 1968.

### When did a dog help a president?
While Richard Nixon was running for vice-president in 1952, he had to defend himself against a charge of accepting gifts of money while he was a senator. On television he gained public support by admitting to receiving just one gift—a dog named Checkers.

### Who was born at an inn?
Andrew Johnson was born in the winter of 1808 in a log cabin in the grounds of an inn, where his father worked as a porter. He grew up in extreme poverty.

### Which presidents were related?

Three sets of presidents have been related. John Quincy Adams was one of four children of John Adams. Benjamin Harrison was one of 13 children of John Scott Harrison, who was one of nine children of William Henry Harrison. Theodore Roosevelt was a fifth cousin of Franklin D. Roosevelt.

### Who was the first poor president?

The first six presidents all came from well-off families. The father of the seventh, Andrew Jackson, was a poor farmer who had emigrated to the United States from Ireland.

### Which president married his cousin?

In 1905, Franklin D. Roosevelt married Eleanor Roosevelt, his fifth cousin, once removed. She took an active part in politics, and after her husband's death she served as Chair of the United Nations Commission on Human Rights.

### Which presidential family is most famous?

In modern times, it must be the Kennedys. John F. Kennedy's father, Joseph Patrick Kennedy, was a millionaire businessman by the age of 35. Two of his brothers entered politics. Robert F. Kennedy was attorney general and a senator. He was assassinated in 1968. Edward Kennedy was also a senator.

### Who married a rich widow?

In 1659, George Washington married Martha Dandridge Custis, a widow with a large estate known as White House (not the White House). She was said to be the wealthiest widow in Virginia. In 1752, he inherited another fortune, his brother's large estate, called Mount Vernon.

# What did the S. in Harry S. Truman stand for?

NOTHING! S. WAS HIS MIDDLE NAME! TRUMAN'S PARENTS COULD NOT DECIDE between the names Shippe or Solomon, the names of his two grandfathers, so they left it as simply S. instead.

Harry Truman came from a farming background. He became president when Roosevelt died in 1945.

### Who was married twice—to the same wife?

Andrew Jackson. In 1791 he married Rachel Donelson Robards. But the marriage was not legal because Rachel was not divorced from her first husband. They were remarried (properly this time) in 1794.

Calvin Coolidge believed in not interfering with the United States' business. He was also known to be sincere.

### Who advised counting to 10?

Thomas Jefferson, the 3rd president of the United States. In his book entitled *A Decalogue of Canons for Observation in Practical Life* he wrote: "When angry, count to 10 before you speak; if very angry, a hundred."

### What did Lincoln say about fooling people?

"You may fool all the people some of the time; you can even fool some of the people all the time; but you can't fool all of the people all the time."

### How did Washington keep the peace?

In his first speech to the American Congress, in 1790, President Washington said, "To be prepared for war is one of the most effectual means of preserving peace."

George Bush was head of the CIA in 1976—7. He is best-known for taking the U.S. into the Gulf War.

# Which president was really cool?

CALVIN COOLIDGE. "KEEP COOL WITH COOLIDGE" WAS THE SLOGAN USED BY the Republicans during the 1924 presidential election campaign.

### Who advised carrying a big stick?

President Theodore Roosevelt's motto was, "Speak softly and carry a big stick; you will go far." He meant that you should use diplomacy, but be ready to use force if necessary.

### What did Wilson encourage fools to do?

Speak! In a speech in 1919, President Wilson said, "If a man is a fool, the best thing to do is to encourage him to advertise the fact by speaking."

### What was Kennedy's most famous saying?

In his inaugural address in 1961, John F. Kennedy said: "And so, my fellow Americans: Ask not what your country can do for you—ask what you can do for your country."

**What was the
Gettysburg Address?**

It was a speech made by President Abraham Lincoln at the site of the Battle of Gettysburg, Pennsylvania, on November 19, 1863, just after the Civil War ended. It contained just 286 words, yet it is one of the most famous speeches ever made. In it, Lincoln spoke of "Government of the people, by the people, and for the people."

# Who wanted his lips read?

GEORGE BUSH. DURING THE PRESIDENTIAL ELECTION CAMPAIGN IN 1988 he announced: "Read my lips: No new taxes." He was reminded of this when several taxes were raised in 1990.

# Whose heads are carved into a mountain?

FOUR OF THE GREATEST AMERICAN PRESIDENTS ARE REMEMBERED AT MOUNT Rushmore National Memorial in South Dakota. Huge heads of George Washington, Thomas Jefferson, Abraham Lincoln, and Theodore Roosevelt are carved into the granite of Mount Rushmore. Carving started in 1927 and finished in 1941.

**Whose monument stands close to the White House?**
The Washington Monument, dedicated to President George Washington. It is an obelisk 555 ft (170 m) high, with a square base. It was built between 1848 and 1884. Visitors can take an elevator to the top.

Gutzon Borglum did most of the carving at Mount Rushmore, but when he died in 1941 his son took over.

### Which president is remembered at an airport?
John F. Kennedy International Airport, New York City, was named after President Kennedy. John F. Kennedy Airport, in Dallas-Fort Worth is also named after him.

### Why are bears called teddies?
Theodore Roosevelt's nickname was Teddy. In 1902, while on a hunting trip in Mississippi, he refused to shoot a bear cub. This inspired a famous cartoon, which in turn inspired a toy called Teddy's bear.

### Who was known as His Accidency?
John Tyler. He was vice-president to William Henry Harrison. When President Harrison died suddenly, Tyler took over. His opponents did not think he should be president, and called him His Accidency.

### Who was General Mum?
William Henry Harrison. The name was given to him because he stayed mum (quiet) during the election campaign. He won because of the way his supporters criticized his opponent, Martin Van Buren.

### Who is sculpted in bronze?
Thomas Jefferson, the 3rd president and the man who drafted the Declaration of Independence. The Thomas Jefferson Memorial in Washington, D.C. is a classical monument with a bronze figure of Jefferson.

# Which president holds back water?

In 1947, the Boulder Dam on the Colorado River was renamed the Hoover Dam to honor President Herbert Hoover. At 726 ft (221 m) high, it is the highest concrete arch dam in the United States.

### Who was Old Man Eloquent?
John Quincy Adams. He earned the nickname after retiring as president and returning to Congress in the House of Representatives, where he served for 17 years.

### Which president was never afraid?
President Lyndon B. Johnson said of Franklin D. Roosevelt, "He was the one person I ever knew, anywhere, who was never afraid."

The Hoover Dam provides water for southern California, Arizona, and Mexico.

# Index

## AB

## CDE

## FGH

## IJKL

## MNO

## PQR

## STU

## VWXYZ

## ACKNOWLEDGEMENTS
The photographs in this book were supplied by: Camera Press 16 (Karl Schumacher), 18—19 (Robert Jackson/Dallas Times Herald); Corbis 24—25, 26, 28—29; Peter Newark's Pictures 1, 7, 9, 11, 13, 15, 20, 21, 22, 23, 24, 27, 28; Photri 31.